Contents

Fiction
Polar Peril
page 2

Play
Stuck!
page 22

Poem
In the Arctic Night
page 28

Non-fiction
Chilling with Polar Bears
page 30

Written by
Benjamin Hulme-Cross

Illustrated by
Frances Castle

Series editor **Dee Reid**

Before reading
Polar Peril

Characters

| Dr Patel |  Amit |  Rupal |  A stranger |

Tricky words

ch1 p3	noticed	ch3 p11	wrestling
ch1 p5	frowned	ch3 p14	completely
ch1 p6	snowmobile	ch4 p18	lowered
ch2 p10	ignored	ch4 p19	distance

Story starter

Dr Patel was an animal conservationist. Her children, Rupal and Amit, were with her at a research centre in the Arctic. They had borrowed cameras from a TV company to make a film teaching people about polar bears. One day a man drove up on his snowmobile. He seemed very interested in the cameras. Rupal had a bad feeling about the man.

Polar Peril

Chapter One

One morning, a stranger came to the Patels' hut. He seemed very friendly and Dr Patel liked him, but Rupal was not so sure. She noticed the man's eyes light up when he saw their expensive filming gear.

"Wow, you've got some cool gear!" said the man. "I haven't seen cameras as good as these before. I bet they cost a lot of money."

"They are expensive," replied Dr Patel. "We're very lucky. A TV company let us borrow their cameras to film the polar bears. We hope to film a bear and her cubs today. Our film will help teach people about polar bears."

"Great! It's important for people to learn about them!" said the man.
"Yes it is!" said Amit, but Rupal frowned. She had a bad feeling about this man.
"Can I help you carry your gear?" the man asked.
"We'll be fine, thanks," Rupal said quickly, before Dr Patel could answer. She didn't trust him. He seemed far too interested in their cameras.

The man waved goodbye and drove away in his snowmobile.
Soon the Patels were ready to go. They packed up the filming gear and climbed onto their snowmobile. It was time to drive across the snow and find the polar bears!

Chapter Two

A polar bear padded out of her cave and yawned. She sniffed the air and caught the smell of the humans. She had seen these people before. She knew they would not harm her, so she was not afraid. Her twin cubs ran out of the cave and started playing in the snow.

The Patels had named the mother bear Sita. They knelt down in the snow and filmed the cubs playing together while Sita stood guard.

After a few minutes, the mother bear froze. She sniffed the air again.

"Something isn't right," said Amit. "Sita is scared."

Sita quickly called to her cubs and they ran back to the cave.
"Look!" Amit said softly. "Another polar bear!" He pointed to a rock near the cave. A huge male polar bear was standing there.

Sita spotted the male bear at the same time. She roared. The male bear roared too and walked towards Sita. Sita showed her teeth, warning him to keep away from her cubs. The male bear ignored Sita's warning. He charged towards her and growled.

Chapter Three

The two bears were locked in a deadly wrestling match.
"We have to help!" cried Amit.
"You're right. If the male bear hurts Sita, he may kill the cubs," said Dr Patel.
She jumped onto the snowmobile and raced across the snow towards the fighting bears. They didn't notice her at all.
"Mum! Look out!" shouted Rupal.

Just then, the snowmobile hit something in the snow and skidded. It slid along the snow until it got stuck between two rocks.

Dr Patel climbed out of the snowmobile. Amit and Rupal rushed over to help her, leaving their cameras in the snow.

The bears stopped fighting and stared at the Patels and the snowmobile. The male bear wasn't used to seeing humans. He grunted and hurried away. Sita went back inside her cave.

The Patels looked at the snowmobile. It was jammed in between the rocks. They tried pushing it. They tried using the power of the engine. They even tried jumping up and down on it. Nothing worked.
It was completely stuck!

Rupal looked up. She thought she had heard footsteps in the snow. She couldn't see anyone, but she had a strange feeling that they were being watched.

Chapter Four

Dr Patel took out her phone to call for help. "No signal!" she said. "What are we going to do?"

"It's OK, that man is here," said Amit. They turned and saw the man who had visited their hut that morning. He was standing where they had been filming the bears earlier.

"Wait!" Rupal warned. "He's looking through our bags. He's going to steal our filming gear!"

"Look at Sita!" Amit shouted suddenly. The others turned around. Sita was charging across the snow towards them. Dr Patel, Amit and Rupal quickly jumped out of the way. Sita still kept on running. She lowered her head and rammed into the snowmobile. It jumped backwards. Sita had pushed it loose!

Suddenly Sita spotted the thief. She stood up on her back legs and roared. The man looked up. Sita charged towards him. He yelped, ran back to his snowmobile and drove off into the distance.

"Sita was helping us!" Amit cried.

Sita looked towards Amit. Then she turned and headed back to her cave and her cubs.

The Patels packed their bags, climbed onto the snowmobile and drove back to their hut.

"It's strange, isn't it?" said Dr Patel.

"What's strange, Mum?" asked Rupal.

"Well," she said, "I always think that we protect the animals, but sometimes it seems the animals are protecting us!"

Quiz

Text detective

- **p3** What first made Rupal suspicious of the man?
- **p7** Why was Sita not afraid of the Patels?
- **p11** Why did Dr Patel drive her snowmobile towards the polar bears?
- **p18** Why do you think Sita rammed the snowmobile?
- **p19** How do you think the man felt when he saw Sita charging at him?

Word detective

- **p11** Why is the metaphor 'locked in a deadly wrestling match' effective?
- **p14** What is the effect of the repetition of 'They tried'?

What do you think?

Do you think Sita was really protecting the Patels? Why would she do that?

HA! HA!

Q: What's a polar bear's favourite cereal?

A: Ice Krispies!

Before reading
Stuck!

Characters

- **Dr Patel** – an animal conservationist
- **Rupal** – her 10-year-old daughter
- **Amit** – Rupal's 11-year-old brother

Setting the scene

Dr Patel and her children are making a film to help people understand how to save the polar bears. When a male polar bear fights a female called Sita, Dr Patel is afraid he will kill Sita's cubs so she drives the snowmobile towards him. The male polar bear moves away but the snowmobile gets stuck between two rocks. Now the Patels are stuck.

Stuck!

Dr Patel: I can't believe I crashed the snowmobile! Now we are stuck out here.

Rupal: You were really brave trying to scare away that male polar bear.

Amit: The male polar bear could have killed Sita and her cubs if you hadn't stopped him. You saved their lives!

Dr Patel: You're right, but what are we going to do now? It's too far to walk to our hut and my phone has no signal.

Amit: Look! Over there! It's that man we met this morning. What is he doing?

Rupal: I can't tell from here.

Dr Patel: If his snowmobile is there, he can rescue us.

Rupal: No, Mum! I don't want him to help us. I don't trust him.

Amit: You don't trust anyone!

Rupal: There is something not quite right about him. I can feel it.

Dr Patel: Well, we are stuck out here. We have to ask him for help.

Amit: Wait! He's looking in our bags. I think he's trying to steal our cameras.

Rupal: I knew there was something not quite right about him.

Amit: *(shouting)* Hey! What do you think you are doing?

Rupal: *(shouting)* Stop it!

Amit: *(shouting)* STOP!

Dr Patel: He can't hear us from over here.

Rupal: We have to stop him!

Dr Patel: How? We don't know what he might do. He could be really dangerous.

Amit: What should we do?

Rupal: I've got an idea. Why don't we take his snowmobile? Then we can get back to the hut. He won't get far if he has to carry our cameras.

Amit: Good idea!

Rupal: Come on, Mum!

Dr Patel: No! If we take his snowmobile, we will be stealing. That is not right.

Rupal: What are we going to do then?

Amit: Wait! Sita is coming over. She is going to attack! I can tell.

Dr Patel: We have to get away from here! Sita might attack us.

Amit: No, she won't attack us. She trusts us.

Rupal: Amit is right. Sita is charging at that man.

Dr Patel: Look! He's running away!

Amit, **Rupal** and **Dr Patel:** *(shouting)*
                              WELL DONE, SITA!

Quiz

Play detective

- **p23** What does Rupal say to make Dr Patel feel better?
- **p24** Why is the word 'shouting' in brackets and italics?
- **p25** Why won't Dr Patel take the man's snowmobile?
- **p26** What evidence is there that Amit can understand animals?
- **p26** Which verb does Rupal use to describe Sita's attack?

Before reading
In the Arctic Night

Setting the scene

Polar bears live in the Arctic. At night, light from the stars shining in the clear skies reflects off the ice to give a white glow. The white fur of the polar bear blends into the snowy background.

Poem top tip

Look for powerful verbs which describe how the polar bears move. Look at the rhyming words at the end of the lines. Can you see a pattern?

Quiz

Poem detective

- What is the rhyming pattern of the poem?
- What adjective is used to describe the polar bears?
- Find two words that describe how the polar bears move.
- Find a simile. Why is it a good simile?

In the Arctic Night

Powerful polar bears
with coats snow-white
roam the shining ice
in the Arctic night.

All is white
in the Arctic night.

Powerful polar bears
hardly show
in their striking coats
as white as snow.

All is white
in the Arctic night.

Powerful polar bears
slide in the snow
in the Arctic dark
as the sharp winds blow.

All is white
in the Arctic night.

Powerful polar bears
with coats snow-white
prowling round
in the Arctic night.

by Celia Warren

Before reading
Chilling with Polar Bears

Find out about

- How polar bears survive in the Arctic
- What prey polar bears hunt
- The effect of climate change on polar bears

Tricky words

p31	weigh	p36	temperatures
p34	breathe	p38	scientists
p35	prey	p38	endangered

Text starter

Polar bears live in and around the Arctic. They spend a lot of their time on the ice and in the sea. They hunt seals and also foxes and deer. The ice in the Arctic is melting and polar bears are finding it harder to survive.

Chilling with Polar Bears

Bear Facts

- Some polar bears weigh over 1000 kg.
- An adult polar bear's paws are around 30 cm wide.
- Polar bears can run faster than athletes!

Where Do They Live?

Polar bears live in and around the Arctic. They spend a lot of their time on the ice. They can walk on the ice without slipping over because they have thick pads on their paws.

Polar bears also spend lots of time in the sea. One polar bear swam over 350 km in ten days. That is over 14 000 lengths of a swimming pool!

How Do Polar Bears Hunt?

Polar bears hunt seals. They can smell seals from over 30 km away.

Seals have to come up from the sea to breathe. The polar bear waits by the edge of the ice until a seal comes to the surface. Then the polar bear scoops the seal out with its strong front legs and paws.

A polar bear hunting for a seal

Polar bears creep up to their prey very slowly. When they are close, they pounce on their prey and kill it.

In the summer, a lot of the ice melts and polar bears have to live on land. This means they can't hunt seals. Polar bears eat foxes and deer instead. They also climb cliffs to hunt birds!

A polar bear hunting for birds on a cliff

Keeping Warm

Polar bears live in temperatures as cold as -40°C. That is colder than a freezer! Polar bears have lots of things that help them stay warm:

- They have a layer of fat that is over 10 cm thick. This is called blubber.
- They have tough skin.
- They have long, thick fur.

Staying Cool

Keeping cool is more of a problem for polar bears than staying warm. Polar bears are built for the cold, but temperatures can reach as high as 30°C in the summer.

So how do polar bears stay cool?

- They walk very slowly.
- They swim in the sea.
- They roll in the snow.

Climate Change

The world is warming up. Winters are warmer and summers are longer. This means that more ice melts and polar bears have fewer places to live. There is also less time for them to hunt seals. This means polar bears are finding it harder to survive. Scientists say that by 2050 there might not be any polar bears left. This is why polar bears are an endangered species.

Quiz

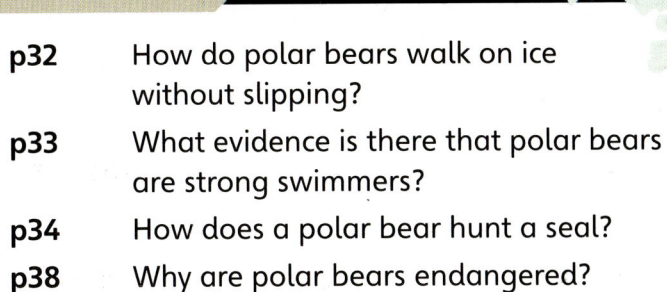

Text detective

p32 How do polar bears walk on ice without slipping?

p33 What evidence is there that polar bears are strong swimmers?

p34 How does a polar bear hunt a seal?

p38 Why are polar bears endangered?

Non-fiction features

p32 What caption would you add to this photo?

p36–37 How does the layout of the pages help you to remember the facts?

What do you think?

Would it matter if there were no polar bears after 2050? Why do you think this? What can we do to help polar bears survive?

HA! HA!

Q: What is white and furry and shaped like a tooth?

A: A molar bear!

Published by Pearson Education Limited, a company incorporated in England and Wales, having its registered office at Edinburgh Gate, Harlow, Essex, CM20 2JE.
Registered company number: 872828

www.pearsonschools.co.uk

Pearson is a registered trademark of Pearson plc

Text © Pearson Education Limited 2013

The rights of Benjamin Hulme-Cross to be identified as the author of this work has been asserted by him in accordance with the Copyright, Designs and Patents Act 1988.

First published 2013

18 17 16 15 14 13
10 9 8 7 6 5 4 3 2 1

British Library Cataloguing in Publication Data is available from the British Library on request.

ISBN: 978 0 435 15240 6

Copyright notice
All rights reserved. No part of this publication may be reproduced in any form or by any means (including photocopying or storing it in any medium by electronic means and whether or not transiently or incidentally to some other use of this publication) without the written permission of the copyright owner, except in accordance with the provisions of the Copyright, Designs and Patents Act 1988 or under the terms of a licence issued by the Copyright Licensing agency, Saffron House, 6-10 Kirby Street, London ECIN 8TS (www.cla.co.uk). Applications for the copyright owner's written permission should be addressed to the publisher.

Designed by Bigtop
Original illustrations © Frances Castle 2013
Illustrated by Frances Castle
Printed and bound in Malaysia (CTP-PPSB)
Font © Pearson Education Ltd
Teaching notes by Dee Reid

Acknowledgements
We would like to thank the following schools for their invaluable help in the development and trialling of this course:
Callicroft Primary School, Bristol; Castlehill Primary School, Fife; Elmlea Junior School, Bristol; Lancaster School, Essex; Llanidloes School, Powys; Moulton School, Newmarket; Platt C of E Primary School, Kent; Sherborne Abbey CE VC Primary School, Dorset; Upton Junior School, Poole; Whitmore Park School, Coventry.

The author and publisher would like to thank the following individuals and organisations for permission to reproduce photographs:

(Key: b-bottom; c-centre; l-left; r-right; t-top)

Creatas: 31c; Digital Vision: 32b; **Getty Images:** 35b, Daniel J Cox 37, Fred Bruemmer 34b, Paul Nicklen 38b; **Veer/Corbis:** Mirage3 33b

All other images © Pearson Education

In some instances we have been unable to trace the owners of copyright material, and we would appreciate any information that would enable us to do so.